Cupcakes

Bite size treats!

A collection of delicious cupcakes and icing recipes!

(im)PulsePaperbacks

Cupcake crazy!

Who can't remember the fabulous smell of baking cupcakes in the oven when they were little? The anticipation of waiting for them to cool; icing the cakes; the joy of elaborately and proudly decorating them with hundreds 'n' thousands, jelly diamonds, little silver balls; the delight of having a cake all to yourself, no sharing necessary… and then the final satisfaction of eating those scrummy-morsels, which epitomised the meaning of the term 'MORE-ISH'; (who amongst us ever got to gorge ourselves as much as we wanted to, under our parents' watchful eyes?)

Universally appealing, there's something so intrinsically different and magical about them; just the name itself 'cupcakes' has a warm-fuzzy feel to it; as do their namesakes; fairy cakes, (a treat befitting a party of fairies!) and muffins, (I defy anyone not to be tempted by the wonderfully whimsical word 'muffins'). Purists may argue that muffins are indeed different to cupcakes, but for the purposes of this book, let's embrace them as one in the interests of variety and being good to our taste buds.

Traditionally, cupcakes have been the food of young children, with basic flavours and recipes; but their rise in popularity has boomed in the last few decades and cupcakes are now well and truly in the culinary 'in-crowd', with a wide variety of creative, hip, chic and tantalising recipes and wonderfully outlandish creations. Indeed, the retailing of products specifically for cupcakes has gone through the roof; and cooking stores are a veritable wonderland of decorations, utensils, novelty shapes, edible treats and fabulous ideas.

So, more popular than ever, the cupcakes-craze shows no signs of abating; and why would it?

Whether made for afternoon tea, children's parties, a wedding, a birthday or for no special reason at all, cupcakes are quite simply a delicious, versatile and fun way to enjoy cakes.

Cupcakes make us smile and appeal to the side of us that never wants to grow up – the food of Peter Pan himself!

Making them can be as easy, or as complicated as you want them to be… and with delicious recipes and icing ideas, this book is the perfect place to begin your cupcake exploration.

Cupcakes are here to stay…, so go ahead, indulge and enjoy!

Sweetie Cupcakes (24 cupcakes)

Ingredients for cupcakes:

255g/2 1/4 cups of self-raising flour
255g/2 1/4 cups of caster sugar
225g/1 cup of unsalted butter (softened)
4 eggs
1 tsp vanilla extract
3-4 tbsps milk

Method for cupcakes:

1. Preheat the oven to 200C/400F/Gas mark 6. Line a cupcake baking tray with paper liners.

2. Place the butter and sugar in a bowl and mix until creamy. Beat in the eggs, one at a time with a little of the flour.

3. Add the vanilla extract and carefully fold in the rest of the flour, alternating it with the milk until all the ingredients have been mixed.

4. Spoon the mixture into the cupcake tray, up to about 3/4 full. Place in the centre of the oven for 15 minutes. Remove from the oven and allow to cool for 5-10 minutes. Remove the cupcakes from the baking tray and place on a wire rack to cool.

Ingredients for icing:

230g/2 cups of icing sugar
1/2 tsp of pink food colouring (or other colour)
3 tbsps lemon juice
3 1/2 tbsps water
Sweets … Dolly Mixtures, Jelly Tots, Smarties, etc

Method for icing:

1. Place the water, lemon juice, icing sugar and food colouring in a bowl and mix well until smooth. Spread smoothly onto each individual cooled cupcake.

2. Leave for about 1 minute and then top with your chosen sweet-topping.

Light-as-a-Feather Cupcakes (12 cupcakes)

Ingredients:

115g/1 cup of flour
230g/2 cups of sugar
1 tsp baking powder
10 egg whites
55g/1/2 cup of cocoa powder
1 tsp cream of tartar, or white vinegar
1/4 tsp salt
1/2 tsp lemon juice
1 tsp vanilla
1 tsp vanilla extract

Method:

1. Preheat the oven to 170C/325F/Gas mark 3. Line a cupcake baking tray with paper liners.

2. Place the egg whites and salt in a bowl and beat until frothy. Add in the cream of tartar (or white vinegar) and beat the mixture, until stiff. Once stiff, stir in the vanilla, sugar and lemon juice.

3. Place the cocoa powder, flour and baking powder in another mixing bowl and mix. Carefully fold in the egg whites gradually.

4. Spoon the mixture into the cupcake liners, up to about 1/2 full. Place in the oven and bake for about 20 minutes.

5. Remove from the oven and leave to cool for 10 minutes. Transfer onto a cooling rack to cool completely.

Children's 'No-Cooking' Party Cupcakes (18–20)

Ingredients:

225g milk chocolate
110g/1/2 cup of miniature marshmallows
55g/1/4 cup of pecan nuts (chopped)
55g/1/2 cup of desiccated coconut
30g/1/8 cup of butter
Silver decorative balls

Method:

1. Place the marshmallows, pecan nuts and coconut in a large bowl.

2. Break the chocolate into a bowl and add the butter. Place in a saucepan of hot water and heat gently until the chocolate has melted. Leave to cool a little for a couple of minutes.

3. Pour the chocolate over the other ingredients in the large bowl and mix thoroughly. Press into small cupcake cases and put in the refrigerator to set.

Decorate with silver decorative balls and serve!

Blueberry Cupcakes (24 – 28 cupcakes)

Ingredients for cupcakes:

115g/1 cup of flour
225g/1 cup of butter
150g/1 1/3 icing sugar
225g/1 cup of blueberries
225g/1 cup of ground almonds
Zest of 1 lemon
4 egg whites

Ingredients for coloured icing:

230g/2 cups of icing sugar
1/2 tsp violet/purple food colouring
3 tbsps lemon juice
3 1/2 tbsps water

Method for cupcakes:

1. Preheat the oven to 180C/350F/Gas mark 4. Line a cupcake baking tray with paper liners. Beat the egg whites until stiff peaks form and leave to one side.

2. Place the butter and sugar in a bowl and beat until pale and fluffy.

3. Place the flour in a separate bowl and coat the blueberries. Remove the blueberries and place to one side.

4. Add the flour and ground almonds to the butter mixture and combine well. Add in the blueberries and mix in. Once mixed well, carefully fold in the egg whites.

5. Spoon the mixture into the cupcake liners, up to about 1/2 full. Place in the oven and bake for 13-15 minutes.

6. Remove from the oven and leave to cool for 5-10 minutes. Transfer onto a wire cooling rack to cool completely.

Method for icing:

1. Place the water, lemon juice, icing sugar and food colouring in a bowl and mix well. Spread smoothly onto each individual cooled cupcake.

Cherry & Cream Cupcakes (24 cupcakes)

Ingredients for cupcakes:

115g/1 cup of flour
200g/3/4 cup of sugar
4 eggs (separated)
1/4 tsp salt
2 tsps grated orange zest (or lemon if preferred)
1 tsp vanilla

Method for cupcakes:

1. Preheat oven to 190C/375F/Gas mark 5. Line a cupcake baking tray with paper muffin liners. Place the egg whites and salt in a bowl and beat until frothy. Add in 2/3 of the sugar, 1 tbsp at a time, beating well each time. Beat the mixture until soft peaks form.

2. In a separate bowl, beat the egg yolks until they are lemon coloured and thick in consistency. Gradually add in the remaining sugar and beat well. Add in the orange or lemon zest and combine. Carefully fold the egg yolk mixture into the egg white mixture. Then sprinkle the flour over the top and fold in using a wooden spoon.

3. Spoon the mixture into the cupcake liners, up to about 1/2 full. Place in the oven and bake for 10-12 minutes. Remove from the oven and leave to cool for 5-10 minutes. Loosen the sides of the muffin liners and remove the cakes. Transfer onto a cooling rack to cool completely.

Ingredients for sour cream filling:

225ml/1 cup pf sour cream
1 egg (beaten)
1/2 tsp vanilla
1 tbsp sugar
1 tbsp flour with a pinch of salt

Method for sour cream filling:

1. Place the flour, sugar and salt in a small bowl and mix together. Mix in the egg and then carefully stir in the sour cream. Blend the mixture together until smooth. Place the bowl in a pan of hot water and heat on a medium setting for about 10 minutes, (until thickened). Stir in the vanilla and leave to cool.

2. Cut a 1 inch diameter cone-shaped piece out of each of the cooled cupcakes, (about 3/4 inch deep). Fill the centres with the sour cream filling.

Ingredients for topping:

25g broken dark chocolate
1 tbsp butter
285g/2 1/2 cups of sugar
1 tbsp butter
55ml/1/4 cup of water
24 maraschino cherries

Method for topping:

1. Add the butter, chocolate and water to a small bowl. Place the bowl in a pan of hot water and heat until melted – blend the mixture together. Add in the icing sugar, stirring well.

2. Drizzle the topping over the sour cream filling in the cakes and then top off with a cherry!

Strawberry Butterfly Cupcakes (24 cupcakes)

Ingredients for cupcakes:

170g/1 1/2 cup of self raising flour
125g butter (softened)
3 eggs
110ml/1/2 cup of milk
75g/2/3 cup of caster sugar
1 tsp vanilla

Ingredients for topping:

Icing sugar (for dusting)
225g/1 cup of strawberries (sliced)
350g white chocolate (broken into pieces)
300ml/1 1/3 cups of whipping cream

Method for cupcakes:

1. Preheat the oven to 180C/350F/Gas mark 4. Line a cupcake baking tray with paper liners.

2. Place the sugar, butter, milk, eggs and vanilla in a large bowl and beat until combined. Beat with a hand-mixer on high speed for 3 minutes, (stopping after each minute to scrape the sides of the bowl).

3. Once the mixture is pale and smooth, spoon the mixture into the cupcake liners, up to about 1/2 full. Place in the oven and bake for 15 minutes. Remove from the oven and leave to cool for 5-10 minutes. Transfer onto a wire cooling rack to cool completely.

Method for topping:

1. Place the chocolate and 55ml/1/4 cup of cream in a saucepan and heat over a medium heat. Stir continuously until the chocolate melts. Leave to cool to room temperature.

2. Place the remaining cream in a bowl and beat with a hand mixer on a medium speed, until soft peaks form. Carefully fold in the chocolate mix into the cream, until well mixed.

3. Using a small, sharp knife cut a circle from the top of each cake and cut the circles in two.

4. Fill the holes created in the cakes with the white chocolate mix and carefully place the two cake-top halves on top; like wings. Top with a strawberry slice and finish with a dusting of icing sugar.

Black Forest Cupcakes (24 cupcakes)

Ingredients for cupcakes:
200g dark chocolate (70% cocoa)
300g/1 1/3 cups of butter (cut into pieces)
900g/4 cups of pitted cherries in syrup
310g/2 3/4 cups of flour
575g/5 cups of caster sugar
110ml/1/2 cup of cherry brandy
2 eggs
4 tbsps self-raising flour
4 tbsps cocoa powder

Ingredients for topping:
200g dark chocolate (70% cocoa powder)
4 tsp cherry brandy
300ml/1 1/3 cups of thick cream, whipped

Method for cupcakes:
1. Preheat the oven to 170C/335F/Gas mark 3-4. Line a cupcake baking tray with paper liners.

2. Drain the cherries, but keep the syrup to one side. Place 1/2 cup of cherries and 1/2 cup of syrup in a food processor and blend until smooth. Cut the remaining cherries in half and put to one side.

3. Place the butter, sugar, cherry brandy, chocolate and pureed cherry mixture into a saucepan. Stir and heat over a medium heat, until the chocolate has completely melted. Pour into a large bowl and leave to cool for 20 minutes.

4. Sift the flours and cocoa into a bowl, gradually add to the wet mixture and whisk until smooth. Whisk in the eggs.

5. Spoon the mixture into the cupcake tray, up to about 3/4 full. Place in the centre of the oven for 40 minutes.

6. Remove from the oven and allow to cool for 5-10 minutes. Remove the cupcakes from the baking tray and place on a wire rack to cool.

Method for topping:
1. Place the whipped cream in a bowl and stir in the cherry brandy. Place a few of the cherry halves on top of each cupcake and top this with some of the brandy/cream.

2. Using a potato peeler, scrape along the side of the block of chocolate and decorate each cake with the chocolate curls.

Pink Champagne (14-16 cupcakes)

Ingredients for the cupcakes:
110g/1/2 cup of Pink Champagne
110g/1/2 cup castor sugar
110g/1/2 cup butter or margarine
110g/1 cup self-raising flour
1 tsp of baking powder
2 eggs

Ingredients for the topping:
225g/1 cup of cream cheese
55g/1/4 cup of unsalted butter
165g/3/4 cup of icing sugar
1/2 tsp red food colouring

Method for the cupcakes:
1. Preheat the oven to 190C/375F/Gas mark 5. Line a cupcake baking tray with paper liners. Cream together the butter and sugar. Add the eggs one at a time and beat well, then add the Champagne.

2. Sieve in the flour and baking powder and mix well. Spoon the mixture into the cupcake tray, up to about 1/2 full. Place in the centre of the oven for 10-12 minutes. Remove from the oven and allow to cool for 5-10 minutes. Remove the cupcakes from the baking tray and place on a wire rack to cool.

Method for the topping:
1. Combine the cream cheese, butter and icing sugar in a bowl and whisk until smooth. Spread over each cake and leave to set.

Orange Cupcakes (16-20 cupcakes)

Ingredients for cupcakes:

200g/1 3/4 cups of flour
115g/1 cup of sugar
110g/1/2 cup of softened butter
2 eggs (separated)
1 tsp vanilla
2 1/2 tsps baking powder
1/4 tsp salt
110ml/1/2 cup of orange juice

Ingredients for orange icing:

1 tbsp grated orange rind
170g/1 1/2 cups of icing sugar
3 tbsps soft butter
2 tbsps orange juice

Method for cupcakes:

1. Preheat oven to 180C/350F/Gas mark 4. Line a cupcake baking tray with paper liners. Place the butter, egg yolks, sugar and vanilla in a large bowl and mix well until creamy.

2. In another bowl add the baking powder, salt and flour and stir together. Slowly add the ingredients into the creamed egg yolk mixture, alternating with a little orange juice each time until all the ingredients are combined.

3. Beat the egg whites and fold carefully into the mixture. Spoon the mixture into the cupcake liners, up to about 2/3 full. Place in the oven and bake for around 15-20 minutes. Remove from the oven and leave to cool for 5-10 minutes. Transfer onto a cooling rack to cool completely.

Method for icing:

1. Place all the icing ingredients into a bowl mix well. Wait until the icing stiffens a little, just enough to spread onto the cakes.

NB. If the mixture is too thick, stir in another tbsp orange juice.

Coconut Cupcakes (18-20 cupcakes)

Ingredients for cupcakes:

15g/1 cup of sugar
140g/1 1/4 cup of flour
40g/1/3 cup of cocoa powder
110ml/1/2 cup of vegetable oil
1 large egg
1 1/2 tsps baking soda
170ml/3/4 cup of water
1 tsp vanilla

Ingredients for filling:

225g cream cheese
40g/1/3 cup of sugar
1 egg
55g/1/2 cup of sweetened coconut flakes

Method for cupcakes:

1. Preheat the oven to 180C/350F/Gas mark 4. Line a cupcake baking tray with paper liners.

2. Place the sugar, flour, cocoa, baking soda, water, egg, oil and vanilla in a large bowl and beat together until smooth.

3. Spoon the mixture into the cupcake liners, up to about 1/2 full.

Method for filling:

1. Place the cream cheese, egg and sugar in a bowl and beat well. Stir in the coconut flakes and mix well.

2. Spoon 1 tbsp filling on top of the chocolate mixture in the cupcake liners. Place in the oven and bake for 25 minutes. Remove from the oven and leave to cool for 5-10 minutes.

3. Transfer onto a wire cooling rack to cool completely. Sprinkle over with a little coconut, if desired.

Banana Cupcakes (24–28 cupcakes)

Ingredients:

255g/2 1/4 cups of flour (sifted)
110g/1/2 cup of unsalted butter (softened)
2 ripe bananas (mashed)
55ml/1/4 cup of buttermilk
2 eggs
115g/1 cup of sugar
1 tsp vanilla
1/2 tsp baking soda
2 1/2 tsps baking powder
1/4 tsp salt

Method:

1. Preheat oven to 190C/375F/Gas mark 5. Line a cupcake baking tray with paper liners.

2. Sift the flour, baking soda, baking powder, sugar and salt into a bowl and mix together.

3. Place the butter and vanilla in another bowl and blend together until a creamy consistency.

4. Gradually add the sugar, beating the mixture until light and fluffy. Add in the eggs, one at a time, beating them well each time.

5. Add in a little of the buttermilk, then a little of the dry mixture, followed by some of the mashed banana to the creamed mixture – beat well after each new ingredient and repeat the alternating process until all the ingredients are combined.

6. Spoon the mixture into the cupcake liners, up to about 1/2 full. Place in the oven and bake for about 20 minutes.

7. Remove from the oven and leave to cool for 5-10 minutes. Transfer onto a cooling rack to cool completely.

Two-Tone Cupcakes (32 cupcakes)

Ingredients for cupcakes:

200g/1 3/4 cups of flour
230g/2 cups of sugar
85g/3/4 cup of unsweetened cocoa powder
1 tsp baking powder
2 tsps baking soda
225ml/1 cup of buttermilk
110ml/1/2 cup of vegetable oil
1 tsp vanilla
225ml/1 cup of boiling water
1 tsp salt
2 eggs

Ingredients for vanilla icing:

110g/1/2 cup of butter (softened)
2 tsps vanilla
460g/4 cups of icing sugar
3-4 tbsps milk

Method for cupcakes:

1. Preheat the oven to 180C/350F/Gas mark 4. Line a cupcake baking tray with paper liners. Place all of the dry ingredients in a large mixing bowl and mix together. Add in the eggs, water, oil, buttermilk and vanilla and beat with a hand mixer for 2 minutes, medium speed, (stop half way to scrape the sides of the bowl).

2. Spoon the mixture into the cupcake liners, up to about 1/2 full. Place in the oven for 15-18 minutes. Remove from the oven and cool for 5-10 minutes. Transfer onto a wire cooling rack to cool completely.

Method for icing:

1. Place the butter and vanilla in a bowl and beat together. Add in 1 cup of the icing sugar and beat until the mixture is a creamy consistency.

2. Add in 1 further cup of icing sugar, followed by 1 tbsp of milk. Repeat this process until all the ingredients have been added. Beat until the mixture is spread-able.

3. Spread onto each of the cooled cupcakes and leave to set.

Lemon Cupcakes (24 cupcakes)

Ingredients for cupcakes:
170g/3/4 cup of butter (softened)
170g/3/4 cup of cream cheese (softened)
4 eggs
115g/1 cup of flour (sifted)
75g/2/3 cup of self-raising flour (sifted)
150g/1 1/3 cups of caster sugar
4 tsps finely grated lemon rind

Method for cupcakes:
1. Preheat the oven to 160C/325F/Gas mark 3. Line a cupcake baking tray with paper liners. Place the cream cheese, butter, sugar, lemon rind and eggs and beat until smooth and creamy.

2. Add the flour gradually to the cheese/butter mixture and beat until just combined.

3. Spoon the mixture into the cupcake tray, up to about 3/4 full. Place in the centre of the oven for 25 minutes. Remove from the oven and leave to cool for 5 minutes. Remove the cupcakes from the baking tray and place on a wire rack to cool.

Ingredients for lemon icing:
55g/1/4 cup of butter (softened)
150g/2/3 cup of cream cheese (softened)
345g/3 cups of icing sugar
2 tsps grated lemon rind

Method for icing:
1. Sift the icing sugar into a bowl and add the other ingredients. Beat together well, until smooth and a spreading consistency.

2. Spread over the cakes and leave to set for 10 minutes.

Mint Cupcakes (18-20 cupcakes)

Ingredients:
200g/1 3/4 cups of sugar
345g/3 cups of flour (sifted)
280ml/1 1/4 cups of milk
2 eggs
2 1/2 tsps baking powder
1/2 tsp salt
150g/2/3 cup of butter
1 tsp vanilla extract
1/2 tsp mint extract

Method:
1. Preheat the oven to 180C/350F/Gas mark 4. Line a cupcake baking tray with paper liners. Place the flour, baking soda and salt in a bowl and mix together.

2. Place the butter and sugar in a bowl and beat until creamy. Add in the eggs, one at a time, beating well after each. Stir in the vanilla and mint extracts.

3. Gradually alternate adding in the flour mixture and the milk, beating well after each addition.

4. Spoon the mixture into the cupcake tray, up to about 3/4 full. Place in the centre of the oven for 20-25 minutes.

5. Remove from the oven and leave to cool for 5 minutes. Remove the cupcakes from the baking tray and place on a wire rack to cool.

Chocolate Cupcakes (20-24 cupcakes)

Ingredients:

230g/2 cups of flour
230g/2 cups of sugar
1 tsp salt
2 large eggs
1/2 tsp baking powder
1 tsp baking soda
170ml/3/4 cup of water
170ml/3/4 cup of milk
1 tsp vanilla
110ml/1/2 cup of melted chocolate

Method:

1. Preheat oven to 180C/350F/Gas mark 4. Line a cupcake baking tray with paper liners.

2. Place all the ingredients, (except the melted chocolate), into a large bowl and mix with a hand mixer for 30 seconds, on low speed. Scrape the bowl and mix again, this time at high speed for 2 1/2 minutes.

3. Spoon the mixture into the paper liners, up to about 2/3 full. Place in the centre of the oven for 20 to 25 minutes. Remove from the oven and allow to cool for 5 minutes. Remove the cupcakes, in their paper liners, and place them on a wire rack to cool down completely.

4. Once the cupcakes have cooled, melt the chocolate and allow to cool for one minute, (don't let it set). Top each of the cakes and leave for at least 10 minutes to set.

Luxury Chocolate Cupcakes (14-16 cupcakes)

Ingredients for cupcakes:

175g/1 1/2 cups of flour
115g/1 cup of sugar
150g/1 & 1/3 cups of brown sugar
110g/1/2 cup of unsalted butter (softened)
3 eggs
1 tsp vanilla extract
55ml/1/4 cup of single cream
150ml/2/3 cup of milk
2 tbsps cocoa powder
1 pack instant hot chocolate
1 tsp baking powder
1/2 tsp bicarbonate of soda

Method for cupcakes:

1. Preheat the oven to 180C/350F/Gas mark 4. Line a cupcake baking tray with paper liners. Place the butter and sugars in a bowl and beat thoroughly until light and creamy. Add in the eggs, one at a time, beating well and then the vanilla extract.

2. Stir in the rest of the ingredients, mixing well until a smooth and even consistency.

3. Spoon the mixture into the cupcake tray, up to about 1/2 full. Place in the centre of the oven for 18-20 minutes. Remove from the oven and allow to cool for 5-10 minutes. Remove the cupcakes from the baking tray and place on a wire rack to cool.

Ingredients for filling:

110g luxury dark chocolate
55g/1/2 cup of light brown sugar
225ml/1 cup of whipping cream
1 tsp vanilla extract
1 packet instant hot chocolate

Method for filling:

1. Break the chocolate into a glass bowl and place in a saucepan of simmering water. Once the chocolate is melted, remove from the heat and leave to cool down a little, (but not too cold).

2. Place the whipping cream and sugar in a large bowl and mix with a hand-mixer on high speed, until the cream thickens.

3. Add the remaining ingredients and mix on high for 2 minutes, scraping the bowl intermittently. Once mixed, stir in the melted chocolate and then chill in the refrigerator.

4. Using a sharp knife, or melon baler, remove a circle from the top/centre of each cupcake. Spoon some of the filling into the freshly created hole and replace the cupcake tops.

Ingredients for dark chocolate icing:

100g luxury dark chocolate
55g/1/4 cup of unsalted butter
55g/1/2 cup of light brown sugar
225ml/1 cup of whipping cream
1 tsp vanilla extract
1 packet instant hot chocolate

Method for icing:

1. Break the chocolate into a glass bowl and place in a saucepan of simmering water. Once the chocolate is melted, remove from the heat and leave to cool down a little, (but not too cold).

2. Place the butter in a large bowl and beat until fluffy. Add in the whipping cream and sugar and mix with a hand-mixer on high speed, until the cream thickens.

3. Add the remaining ingredients and mix on high for 2 minutes, scraping the bowl intermittently. Once mixed, stir in the melted chocolate and then leave for a couple of minutes to set slightly.

4. Spread the icing carefully, then top with chocolate sprinkles, chocolate buttons, Maltesers; or any other preferred chocolate!

Milk Chocolate Cupcakes (20-24 cupcakes)

Ingredient for cupcakes:

170g/1 1/2 cup of flour
75g/2/3 cup of cocoa powder
170g/1 1/2 cups of sugar
2 eggs
1 tsp baking soda
110g/1/2 cup of butter (softened)
225ml/1 cup of milk
1 tsp vanilla
1/2 tsp salt

Method for cupcakes:

1. Preheat the oven to 180C/350F/Gas mark 4. Line a cupcake baking tray with paper liners. Place the cocoa powder, flour, baking soda and salt in a bowl and mix together.

2. Place the sugar, vanilla, eggs and butter in a large bowl and beat together. Carefully beat in the flour/cocoa mixture. Spoon the mixture into the cupcake liners, up to about 1/2 full. Place in the oven and bake for 20 minutes. Remove from the oven and leave to cool for 5-10 minutes. Transfer onto a wire cooling rack to cool completely.

Ingredients for milk chocolate icing:

350g milk chocolate (broken into pieces)
6 tbsps butter (softened)
285g/2 1/2 cups of icing sugar
55ml/1/4 cup of milk
1 tsp vanilla

Method for icing:

1. Place the milk chocolate in a small bowl and cover with the vegetable oil. Place in a pan of hot water and heat over a medium heat, stirring the chocolate until it melts.

2. Transfer the mixture to a large bowl and gradually beat in the icing sugar, alternating it with milk. Finally, stir in the vanilla. Spread on each of the cooled cupcakes and leave to set.

Dark Chocolate Cupcakes (24 cupcakes)

Ingredients:

150g/1 & 1/3 cup of flour
230g/2 cups of sugar
225g/1 cup of butter (softened)
4 eggs (beaten)
110ml/1/2 cup of milk
6oz dark chocolate (70%)
1 1/2 tsp vanilla extract
1/4 tsp orange oil
1/2 tsp baking powder
1/4 tsp salt

Method:

1. Preheat the oven to 180C/350F/Gas mark 4. Line a cupcake baking tray with paper liners. Place the butter and sugar in a bowl and beat until creamy. Add in the eggs, one at a time, beating well each time.

2. Break the chocolate into a bowl and place in a bowl of hot water. Heat over a medium heat until the chocolate is melted. Remove from the heat.

3. Add in the milk, vanilla, chocolate and vanilla oil; mixing well each time. Fold in the baking powder, flour and salt and mix well, until smooth and blended.

4. Spoon the mixture into the cupcake tray, up to about 3/4 full. Place in the centre of the oven for 20-25 minutes. Remove from the oven and leave to cool for 5 minutes. Remove the cupcakes from the baking tray and place on a wire rack to cool

Chocolate Butter Cream (24 cupcakes)

510g/4 1/2 cups of icing sugar
300g/1 & 1/3 cup of butter (softened)
4 tbsp cocoa powder
4 tsp hot water

Method:

Place the butter and sugar in a bowl and beat thoroughly. Place the cocoa powder and water in a bowl and combine. Beat into the butter/sugar mixture until smooth and creamy. Spread over the cooled cupcakes.

Coconut Icing (14-16 cupcakes)

175g dark chocolate (broken into pieces)
165ml/3/4 cup of evaporated milk
115g/1 cup of sugar
1/2 tsp coconut extract
6 tbsp butter (cut into pieces)

Method:

1. Place the chocolate in a bowl and put to one side. Pour the evaporated milk into a pan and heat until just simmering.

2. Remove from the heat and pour over the chocolate. Leave for 8-10 minutes and then mix in a food processor well until smooth.

3. Add in the sugar and coconut extract and mix. Once mixed, gradually, piece by piece, add in the butter. Process until the mixture thickens to spreading, or piping consistency.

4. Pour out of the processor into a bowl and leave for a few minutes to firm a little, (pop in the fridge if the room is too warm). Spread, or pipe over the cupcakes and leave to set for 20 minutes before serving.

Lemon Icing (24 cupcakes)

55g/1/4 cup of butter (softened)
170g/3/4 cup of cream cheese (softened)
345g/3 cups of icing sugar
2 tsps grated lemon rind

Method:

Sift the icing sugar into a bowl and add the other ingredients. Beat together well, until smooth. Spread over the cooled cupcakes.

Marshmallow Icing (12 cupcakes)

2 tbsp unsalted butter
345g/3 cups of mini marshmallows
55ml/1/4 cup of double cream

Method:

Place all the ingredients in a saucepan and heat over a low heat. Stir continuously until all the ingredients are melted and combined. Leave to cool until a spreading consistency.

Royal White Icing (24 cupcakes)

690g/6 cups of icing sugar
4 large egg whites
1 1/2 tsp lemon juice

Method:

Place the icing sugar and egg whites in a bowl and whisk with an electric hand-mixer on medium speed; for about 5 minutes, (the mixture should become thick and shiny). Whisk in the lemon juice and beat for a few more minutes, until the mixture reaches a spreading consistency.

Coloured Icing (24–28 cupcakes)

230g/2 cups of icing sugar
1/2 tsp chosen food colouring
3 tbsps lemon juice
3 1/2 tbsps water

Method:

Place the water, lemon juice, icing sugar and food colouring in a bowl and mix well. Spread smoothly onto each individual cooled cupcake.

Cream Cheese Icing (20–24 cupcakes)

225g/1 cup of cream cheese
55g/1/4 cup of unsalted butter
165g/3/4 cup of icing sugar

Method:

Combine the cream cheese, butter and icing sugar in a bowl and whisk until smooth. Spread over each cake and leave to set.

Coffee Icing (24 cupcakes)

3 tsps instant coffee granules
115g/1 cup of white icing
Powdered cocoa (to dust)

Method:

Place the vanilla, instant coffee granules and 1 tsp warm water in a bowl and stir until the coffee has dissolved. Stir in the white icing sugar and blend well. Spread over each cupcake. Dust with powdered cocoa powder.

Amaretto Icing (24 cupcakes)

3 tbsps Amaretto
345g/3 cups of icing sugar
4 tbsps whipping cream
55g/1/4 cup of butter

Method:

Place the butter and sugar in a bowl and beat well. Add in the cream and amaretto and beat until smooth. Leave to set a little for a few minutes, or until the mixture is a good spreading consistency. Spread over each of the cupcakes.

Banana Icing (28 cupcakes)

110g/1/2 cup of mashed bananas
1/2 tsp lemon juice
230g/2 cups of icing sugar

Method:

Place the mashed banana, lemon juice and icing sugar in a bowl and whisk until smooth, and a spreading consistency. Spread over each individual cupcake.

Butterscotch Glaze (12 cupcakes)

115g/1 cup of icing sugar
55g/1/4 cup of butter
30g/1/4 cup of brown sugar
1 tsp rum extract (or vanilla if preferred)
2 tbsps milk

Method:

Place the brown sugar, milk and butter in a saucepan and bring to the boil. Remove from the heat. Add the sugar and rum extract and beat the mixture until smooth. Drizzle over the cooled cupcakes.

NB. If glaze is too thick, just add a little more milk.

Butterscotch Icing (24 cupcakes)

250g butterscotch (broken)
110ml/1/2 cup of double cream

Method:

Place the butterscotch in a bowl and place cream in a pan, over a medium heat and heat until almost boiling.

Pour the cream over the butterscotch and leave to soften. Whisk the mixture until smooth and leave to cool. Whisk again, until light and fluffy and spread over each cupcake.

Peanut Butter Icing (18 cupcakes)

75ml/1/3 cup of double cream
1/4 tsp salt
115g/1 cup of icing sugar
225g/1 cup of smooth peanut butter
5 tbsps unsalted butter (softened)
1 tsp vanilla extract

Method:

Place the icing sugar, butter, peanut butter, salt and vanilla in a bowl and mix until creamy with an electric hand-mixer, (paddle attachment), on low speed. Scrape the sides of the bowl intermittently.

Add in the cream and beat on high speed until the mixture is smooth and light. Spread over the cooled cupcakes.

Raspberry Icing (12 cupcakes)

55g/1/4 cup of fresh raspberries (crushed)
2 tsps lemon juice
230g/2 cups of icing sugar (sifted)

Method:

Place the crushed raspberries in a bowl and add the sugar; mix well. Add in the lemon juice and mix until the mixture is of spreading consistency, this should be quite thin. Spread over the cooled cupcakes.

Easter-Nest Cupcakes (20-24 cupcakes)

Ingredients for cupcakes:

170g/1 1/2 cup of flour
75g/2/3 cup of cocoa powder
170g/1 1/2 cups of sugar
2 eggs
1 tsp baking soda
110g/1/2 cup of butter (softened)
225ml/1 cup of milk
1 tsp vanilla
1/2 tsp salt

Ingredients for milk chocolate icing topping:

350g milk chocolate (broken into pieces)
6 tbsps butter (softened)
285g/2 1/2cups of icing sugar
55ml/1/4 cup of milk
1 tsp vanilla
12 chocolate flake bars
Large pack of mini-chocolate eggs

Method for cupcakes:

1. Preheat the oven to 180C/350F/Gas mark 4. Line a cupcake baking tray with paper liners. Place the cocoa powder, flour, baking soda and salt in a bowl and mix together.

2. Place the sugar, vanilla, eggs and butter in a large bowl and beat together. Carefully beat in the flour/cocoa mixture.

3. Spoon the mixture into the cupcake liners, up to about 1/2 full. Place in the oven and bake for 20 minutes. Remove from the oven and leave to cool for 5-10 minutes. Transfer onto a wire cooling rack to cool completely.

Method for icing:

1. Place the milk chocolate in a small bowl and cover with the vegetable oil. Place in a pan of hot water and heat over a medium heat, stirring the chocolate until it melts.

2. Transfer the mixture to a large bowl and gradually beat in the icing sugar, alternating it with milk. Finally, stir in the vanilla. Spread generously on each of the cooled cupcakes.

3. Cut each of the chocolate flakes in half and then cut them in half, length ways. Arrange the pieces of flake around the top of each egg, giving a nest-like appearance, (use the icing to stick parts together, if needed). Place 3 mini-eggs in the centre of each arrangement. To make a really special effort, buy some fluffy decorative 'chicks' and place one on each cake.

Spider's Web Cupcakes (24 cupcakes)

Ingredients for cupcakes:

115g/1 cup of self-raising flour
115g/1 cup of flour
55g/1/4 cup of pecan nuts (chopped)
225ml/1 cup of vegetable oil
175g/1 1/2 cups of soft brown sugar
4 eggs
300g/1 1/3 cup of pumpkin (grated finely)
2 tsps cinnamon
1 tsp baking soda
1 tsp cinnamon
2 tbsps golden syrup

Method for cupcakes:

1. Preheat the oven to 160C/325F/Gas mark 3. Line a cupcake baking tray with paper liners.

2. Sift the flours, ginger, baking soda and cinnamon into a large bowl and mix together.

3. Place the vegetable oil, eggs, sugar and golden syrup in a large jug and whisk together. Pour into the flour mixture and beat together well. Add the pecans and pumpkin and stir in.

4. Spoon the mixture into the cupcake tray, up to about 3/4 full. Place in the centre of the oven for 25-30 minutes, or until golden brown.

5. Remove from the oven and leave to cool for 5 minutes. Remove the cupcakes from the baking tray and place on a wire rack to cool.

Ingredients for icing:

225g dark chocolate (broken into pieces)
500g/4 1/3 cups of icing sugar
4 large egg whites
1 1/2 tsps lemon juice

Method for icing:

1. Place the icing sugar and egg whites in a bowl and whisk with an electric hand-mixer on medium speed; for about 5 minutes, (the mixture should become thick and shiny).

2. Whisk in the lemon juice and beat for a few more minutes, until the mixture reaches a spreading consistency. Spread thinly over each of the cooled cupcakes. Break the chocolate into a small bowl and place in a saucepan of hot water. Heat over a medium heat until the chocolate is melted.

3. Using a skewer, teaspoon or other appropriate implement – drizzle the chocolate in a spiral over each cake. Using a clean skewer, start from the centre and drag down in a straight line to the outer edge. Repeat this a number of times on each cake to give a 'spider's web' effect. Leave to set before serving.

Christmas Cupcakes (24 cupcakes)

Ingredients for cupcakes:

225g/1 cup of margarine
230g/2 cups of self-raising flour
3 tbsps cocoa powder
230g/2 cups of caster sugar
4 eggs (beaten)
2 tsps baking powder
10 tbsps milk

Ingredients for icing:

230g/2 cups of icing sugar
1/2 tsp black food colouring
3 tbsps lemon juice
3 1/2 tbsps water
Edible, decorative silver balls
Silver tinsel (to decorate)

Method for cupcakes:

1. Preheat the oven to 160C/325F/Gas mark 3. Line a cupcake baking tray with paper liners. Sift the flour, baking powder and cocoa powder into a bowl and mix together. Add in the caster sugar, margarine, milk and eggs and beat together well.

2. Spoon the mixture into the cupcake tray, up to about 3/4 full. Place in the centre of the oven for 25-30 minutes, or until golden brown.

3. Remove from the oven and leave to cool for 5 minutes. Remove the cupcakes from the baking tray and place on a wire rack to cool.

Method for icing:

1. Place the water, lemon juice, icing sugar and food colouring in a bowl and mix well. Spread smoothly onto each individual cooled cupcake.

2. Scatter the cupcakes with the decorative silver balls and leave to set. Serve on a plate and surround with the silver tinsel.

Christmas Holly Cupcakes (24 cupcakes)

Ingredients for cupcakes:

315g/2 3/4 cups of flour
225g/1 cup of unsalted butter (softened)
315g/2 3/4 cups of dark brown sugar
4 eggs
2 tsps baking powder
1 tsp baking soda
6 tbsps sour cream
1 tsp mixed spice
Pinch of salt
150g dark chocolate (broken)
2 tsps instant coffee granules
225ml/1 cup of boiling water

Method for cupcakes:

1. Preheat the oven to 200C/400F/Gas mark 6. Line a cupcake baking tray with paper liners. Place the baking powder, mixed spice, flour, baking soda and salt in a large bowl and mix together.

2. Place the butter and sugar in a bowl and beat until creamy. Add the eggs, one at a time, beating each new addition well. Add 1/3 of the flour mixture, followed by a tbsp of sour cream. Repeat this process until all the flour mixture and sour cream is mixed in.

3. Place the chocolate, instant coffee and water in a saucepan and heat gently over a low heat. Heat until all the chocolate is melted, remove from the heat and fold into the cake batter. The mixture should be quite thin.

4. Spoon the mixture into the cupcake tray, up to about 3/4 full. Place in the centre of the oven for 20 minutes, or until golden brown. Remove from the oven and leave to cool for 5 minutes. Remove the cupcakes from the baking tray and place on a wire rack to cool.

Ingredients for icing:

500g/4 & 1/3 cups of icing sugar
4 large egg whites
1 1/2 tsps lemon juice
2 packets of ready-made green icing
1 holly leaf cutter (small)
60 fresh cranberries

Method for icing:

1. Place the icing sugar and egg whites in a bowl and whisk with an electric hand-mixer on medium speed; for about 5 minutes, (the mixture should become thick and shiny).

2. Whisk in the lemon juice and beat for a few more minutes, until the mixture reaches a spreading consistency. Spread thickly over each of the cooled cupcakes.

3. Roll out the ready-made green icing, (alternatively you can make your own, just add green colouring). Cut out 2 holly leaves for each cake and carefully place over the white icing. Finish off with a couple of fresh cranberries on top, for the holly berries.

The recipes contained in this book are passed on in good faith but the publisher cannot be held responsible for any adverse results. Please be aware that certain recipes may contain nuts. The recipes use both metric and imperial measurements, and the reader should not mix metric and imperial measurements. Spoon measurements are level, teaspoons are assumed to be 5ml, tablespoons 15ml. For other measurements, see chart below. Times given are for guidance only, as preparation techniques may vary and can lead to different cooking times.

Spoons to millilitres

1/2 teaspoon	2.5 ml	1 Tablespoon	15 ml
1 teaspoon	5 ml	2 Tablespoons	30 ml
1-1 1/2 teaspoons	7.5 ml	3 Tablespoons	45 ml
2 teaspoons	10 ml	4 Tablespoons	60 ml

Grams to ounces

10g	0.25oz	225g	8oz
15g	0.38oz	250g	9oz
25g	1oz	275g	10oz
50g	2oz	300g	11oz
75g	3oz	350g	12oz
110g	4oz	375g	13oz
150g	5oz	400g	14oz
175g	6oz	425g	15oz
200g	7oz	450g	16oz

Metric to cups

Description		1 cup
Flour etc	115g	1 cup
Clear honey etc	350g	1 cup
Liquids etc	225ml	1 cup

Liquid measures

5fl oz	1/4 pint	150 ml
7.5fl oz		215 ml
10fl oz	1/2 pint	275 ml
15fl oz		425 ml
20fl oz	1 pint	570 ml
35fl oz		1 litre

This edition first published in 2009 by ImPulse Paperbacks, an imprint of Iron Press Ltd. © Iron Press Ltd 2009 Printed in China